Living in the Land of Miracles

By

Gary Parsons

ISBN: 1-4140-2076-7 (e-book)
ISBN: 1-4140-2075-9 (Paperback)

This book is printed on acid free paper.

1stBooks - rev. 12/03/03

I would like to thank Lillian, Holly, Julie and Dorothy.

From the Author...

As God began to put this book into my spirit, I could not help but look back at my own life. It seems to have been an incredible journey. It took me forty years and eleven months to discover my purpose for living, but I discovered the plans God had for me when I gave my life totally to Him through salvation. My way of living took a one-hundred-eighty degree turn. I was changed forever. For the positive change in my life, I truly give God the glory. I have witnessed many miracles in my lifetime, but the greatest miracle of all was when God saved me and called me into the ministry in November

of 1990.

Table of Contents

Chapter 1

Ingredients for a Miracle

Salvation

The greatest miracle for anyone is the miracle of salvation. No person can come to God unless God seeks you. Luke 19:10 tells us that "For the Son of Man is come to seek and to save that which was lost." (KJV).

God is seeking you out so that He can save you and give you eternal life in heaven with Him. Glory to God! Isn't that awesome? Luke 15:4 asks "What man of you, having a hundred sheep if he lose one of them, doth not leave the ninety and nine in the wilderness, and go after that which is

lost, until he find it?" (KJV)

Diligence

After you are saved and you become a believer in Christ,

then the seeking becomes your responsibility. Hebrews

11:6 confirms that "He (God) is a rewarder of them that

diligently seek Him." (KJV) Here we find that seeking God

will begin to bring the benefits of being a child of God to a

reality. We must diligently seek Him—not talk about

seeking Him, but actually do it. God does honor His word

if we will seek Him the way He says to, and that is

diligently. According to Webster's Dictionary, diligence is

"to show painstaking effort and application in whatever is

undertaken." I must confess, as a pastor and evangelist, that

I see few believers diligently seeking God. We need to get

this into our spirits that God wants to see diligence in our lives today. Diligence is a key ingredient in every area of the believer's life in regard to receiving a miracle. Proverbs 13:4 tells us that "The soul of the sluggard desireth, and hath nothing, but the soul of the diligent shall be made fat." (KJV)

Spiritual Health

God wants you spiritually healthy. Being spiritually healthy will feed your physical body. When you are spiritually healthy, you can cast your cares on God because He cares for you, (1 Peter 5:7). Praise God! The ability to cast your cares upon God comes through knowing the Word of God. Exodus 14:14 tells us that "the Lord shall fight for you." (KJV) When we get this into our spirits, then we can enjoy what God means when He says to cast your cares upon Him.

Faith

Faith is another ingredient in the recipe for a miracle. In the hands of God, faith becomes substance. Substance becomes the source of what your need is. "Now faith is the substance of things hoped for, the evidence of things not seen," Hebrews 11:1. (KJV)

Faith is an act of the mind and heart and we are convinced that what we are believing God for will come to pass. Our faith becomes the title deed of things hoped for. The answer is sure—just as sure as the title deed to your property.

Faith is believing or trusting in the unseen. It is not trust in the unknown because we may know by faith what we cannot see with our eyes or hear with our ears. Faith is being one hundred percent sure that what God says about your situation will take place.

From God's perspective, we already possess His promises. Hebrews 10:23 says, "Let us hold fast the profession of our faith without wavering, (for He is faithful that promised)." (KJV)

Isaiah 53:5 says "with His stripes we are healed." (KJV) Healing and health already belong to the believer. We must plant this into our spirits and not be intimidated by adverse circumstances. Your body may tell you that you are not healed, but if God's word says you are healed, then by faith which is substance, you are healed in Jesus' name. Hebrews 11:3 tells us that "Through faith we understand that the worlds were framed by the word of God." (KJV) The word **understand** means **to know a true fact**. We do not assume that God created the world, but we state the fact that

God created the world. Genesis 1:1 says, "In the beginning God created the Heaven and the earth." (KJV) This is a fact. God did create the world, as it is also fact that by His stripes you are healed. This is a fact—Praise God!

Psalm 33:9 says, "For He spake and it was done; he commanded, and it stood fast." (KJV) As impossible as this verse sounds, it still stands true.

Psalm 103:2-3 tells us, "Bless the Lord, O my soul, and forget not all His benefits: who forgiveth all thine iniquities; who healeth <u>all</u> **(emphasis mine)** thy diseases." (KJV) There are those who do not believe miracles are for us in this day and time. Do not let man's opinion on God's Word weaken your faith. "For the promise is unto you, and to your children, and to all that are far off, even as many as the Lord our God shall call," Acts 2:39. (KJV)

Isaiah 55:11 says, "So shall my Word be that goeth forth out of my mouth: it shall not return unto me void, but it shall accomplish that which I please, and it shall prosper in the thing whereto I sent it." (KJV) God watches over His word to make it come to pass in our lives—Glory to God!

Confession

Faith speaks about something you cannot see with your eyes. Faith makes a positive confession about your situation. Confession is a very important substance in your recipe for a miracle. You confess what God's Word says and not what you are feeling or seeing. There are times in my own life that I do not feel saved even though I haven't fallen into sin, but God's Word says I am saved regardless of what my mind tells me, so I confess that I am saved with my mouth. Revelation 12:11 tells us, "And they overcame him by the blood of the lamb, and by the word of their testimony." (KJV) Faith demands the impossible to come to pass and Jesus' blood puts His stamp of approval on your request. Never speak anything less than the Word of God. Proverbs 6:2 tells us "thou art snared with the words of thy mouth." (KJV)

Begin to quote Psalm 23:1, "The Lord is my shepherd, I shall not want." (KJV) When we begin to acknowledge what God's Word says about us, then we begin to realize that we can have what His Word says we can have. Psalm 37:4 tells us to "Delight thyself also in the Lord; and He shall give thee the desires of thine heart." (KJV) Do you enjoy serving God? Do you enjoy talking about the things of God? If you delight in the things of God, then rest assured that the desires of your heart are coming. Confess daily how you take delight in serving God.

Church Attendance

Is it a delight for you to be faithful to God in church attendance? In order for God to perform His Word in your life, He must see a love in your life or heart for the things that are important to Him. So many "so-called" believers seem to take church attendance lightly, but God looks at church attendance as being very important. God even went so far as to include the importance of the Sabbath in the Ten Commandments. Exodus 20:8 says, "Remember the Sabbath day by keeping it Holy." (NIV) It makes no difference what you think you should be doing on the Lord's day because, as in every case, God has the last word! Hebrews 10:25 tells us "Let us not give up meeting together, as some are in the habit of doing, but let us encourage one another—and all the more as you see the Day approaching." (NIV)

There are those who are unable to be in church because of bad health as well as many other reasons, but if you are able to be in church, God expects you to be there! The way I understand the Bible, to break any of the Ten Commandments is sin, and living in sin will keep you out of Heaven and *could* even keep you from getting your miracle. As we read on in Hebrews, God says if we deliberately keep on sinning after we have received the knowledge of the truth, "…no sacrifice for sins is left, but only a fearful expectation of judgment and of raging fire that will consume the enemies of God," (Heb.10:26-27) (NIV).

Removal of Deception

The devil uses deception as a major tool to keep people living in extremely dangerous circumstances. There are a lot of people who had better wake up and take a good look at the way they are living their lives, because God tells us in Hebrews 10:31 that "It is a dreadful thing to fall into the hands of the living God." (NIV) If there are changes that need to be made in your life, *then make them*! This could be a turning point in your life that could set in motion a much needed miracle in your life.

Unconditional Obedience

God wants you to start lining your life up with His Word. This is what sets in motion the hand of God in your life. First and foremost, God demands unconditional obedience!

Draw Nigh to God

In order to get to this level of obedience, God requires drawing as close to Him as we can. James 4:8 tells us to

"Draw nigh to God, and He will draw nigh to you…" (KJV)

As a pastor and evangelist, I have observed that believers are not drawing nigh to God. Seeking God is a major factor in receiving your miracle. I addressed the importance of seeking God earlier in this book, but this is so important, I must take a deeper look into God's Word.

I must ask the question, how desperate are you to see God intervene in your life? Matthew 7:7-8 says to "Ask and it will be given to you; seek and you will find; knock and the door will be opened to you. For everyone who asks receives; he who seeks finds; and to him who knocks the door will be opened." (NIV) At first glance, these two verses make it sound really easy, but they indicate some persistence. It is that "seek" word that separates believers from their miracles.

Prayer

God wants you to pray often, with intensity. Do not play around in prayer. Prayer is serious business, and God demands that we take prayer seriously. You must not pray with selfish desires or motives. What you pray for must line up with His Word, and at the same time, you must acknowledge your dependence on His Word. Psalm 105:4 tells us to "Seek the Lord, and His strength; seek His face evermore." (KJV) God wants you to ask for supernatural strength and to continue seeking Him. God has given us the Bible, and within the pages of His Word, He gives us valuable information that will literally open heaven's windows in every believer's life. No believer will ever be in any situation that God's Word cannot show him how to be victorious. But in order to be victorious we must do exactly as God's Word instructs us. What I am about to explain to you is extremely important to the receiving of your miracle.

Galatians 6:7 says, "Be not deceived; God is not mocked: for whatsoever a man soweth, that shall he also reap." (KJV) I enjoy pretty flowers around my home, but in order to have pretty flowers, time is required of me, as well as of my wife. Quite frankly, there is a lot of work required to produce a pretty flower garden. Now if I plant a rose bush, I expect that rose bush to come up out of the ground and develop into a beautiful rose bush. I do not plant my rose expecting weeds to grow in its place. I sowed a rose bush, and it will reap roses. In the same manner, God expects believers to sow prayers. God wants believers to diligently pray. God wants to see us pray with intensity and to follow our prayers with unconditional obedience. Many times I wonder if believers realize the importance of a prayer life. I believe that if the church would wake up again and begin to pray with diligence and perseverance, we would experience a mighty move of God, based upon what Luke 6:38 says, "for with the same measure that you use, it will be measured to you." (NIV) As the believer pours out his heart to God, God will with the same measure, pour heavenly blessings on the believer.

The more we seek God, the more benefits and rewards we can expect. Hebrews 11:6 says, "…He is a rewarder of them that diligently seek Him." (KJV) As you seek God, you wake up to the fact that your past failures came your way because of the lack of your knowledge of God. As you pray and study God's Word, you find God working in areas of your life for His good pleasure. Philippians 2:13 says, "For it is God which worketh in you both to will and to do of His good pleasure." (KJV) God works in us. God works through us. God works for us. His overall plan is to operate through us—Wow! As God begins to operate through us and use us like never before, we find ourselves at a new level in Christ, which I call "Living in the Land of Miracles."

Chapter 2

Living in the Land of Miracles

God has given us His Word, the Bible, as a resource to resolve *every* problem we will ever encounter here on planet earth. Please allow me to address the Bible as God's Resource Manual because "resource" means "a source of aid or support which can be drawn upon if needed." No person will ever write a book equivalent to the Bible. If you are not a reader of the world's best selling book, the Bible, you are robbing yourself of God's best for your life.

When you invited Jesus Christ to come into your heart, and asked Christ to forgive you for your sins, He came into your heart and you became <u>at</u> <u>that</u> <u>moment</u> one of God's children. Romans 8:16-17 tells us that "The spirit himself testifies with our spirit that we are God's children. Now if we are children, then we are heirs—heirs of God and co-heirs with Christ." (NIV) Wow! We become an heir of the One who spoke this world into existence. Genesis 1:1, "In the beginning God created the Heavens and the Earth." (KJV) You have become an heir, as a child of God, to everything Christ has.

This sounds good, but if I am going to inherit something, I want to know what I am going to get. First and foremost, we inherit eternal life in heaven with God. He is preparing a mansion for every "faithful" child of God. John 14:2 says "In my Father's house are many rooms; if it were not so, I would have told you. I am going there to prepare a place for you. And if I go and prepare a place for you, I will come back and take you to be with me that you also may be where I am." (NIV) If you are a faithful follower of Jesus Christ, this is your future.

Notice—Jesus called God "My Father." God really does exist. Jesus knew his Father's house. God's house is real. It is a real world that exists in another dimension. The word "mansion" means an abiding place for living. What a hope! This is what God is talking about in Matthew 6:33. "But seek first His kingdom and His righteousness, and all these things will be given to you as well." (NIV) God wants His children to pursue heaven through seeking Him. God wants His children to live holy lives, and as we pursue holiness, everything we need will be given to us. This is *Living in the Land of Miracles*.

However, notice there is a condition.   John 14:15-16 says "If you love me, you will obey what I command. And I will ask the Father, and He will give you another Counselor to be with you forever." (NIV) Jesus said, "if you love me," stressing an ongoing attitude of love and unconditional obedience.   Jesus calls the Holy Spirit "another Counselor," which means one called alongside to help in every situation you encounter in your life. Living in this new dimension spiritually, "the Counselor, the Holy Spirit, whom the Father will send in my name, will teach you all things and will remind you everything I have said to you," John 14:26. (NIV) God has sent His Helper to abide with you, to help in your decisions, to guide your steps while you are here on planet earth.   Proverbs 4:11-13 assures us, "I guide you in the way of wisdom and lead you along straight paths. When you walk, your steps will not be hampered; when you run, you will not stumble. Hold on to instruction. Do not let it go; guard it well, for it is your life." (NIV) God is very interested in your life. He wants to guard your steps. He will even keep you from falling. The key is to possess knowledge of what God says about life. He tells us to hold on to His resources, for His resources are life.

Living life on earth can sometimes become very difficult for the believer. This is why it is very important to stay close to Jesus because He tells us in Psalms 9:9-10, "The Lord is a refuge for the oppressed, a stronghold in times of trouble. Those who know your name will trust in you, for you, Lord, have never forsaken those who seek you." (NIV)

A major factor in your life is prayer. God actually commands us to seek Him and to cast our cares or problems on Him. Psalm 55:22 says to "Cast your cares on the Lord and He will sustain you; He will never let the righteous fall." (NIV) Believe it or not, whatever is going on in your life right now, God will take care of you, but you must give your problem to Jesus and let him keep it. Jesus is our burden bearer. He will come to you in the middle of life's storms and command peace on you. It doesn't make any difference how raging your storm is, Jesus will give you peace. He tells us in John 14:27, "Peace I leave with you; my peace I give you. I do not give to you as the world gives. Do not let your hearts be troubled and do not be afraid." (NIV) God offers us His peace. The world offers a false peace, but God offers sweet peace. If you can only accept the fact that this offer is good for every born again believer, God gives us His peace! Wow!

So very often our peace can be interrupted because of the fear of the unknown. As children of God, we can choose to not allow fear to overtake us. God's Word assures us in Proverbs 3:24-26 "…when you lie down, you will not be afraid; when you lie down, your sleep will be sweet. Have no fear of sudden disaster or of the ruin that overtakes the wicked, for the Lord will be your confidence and will keep your foot from being snared." (NIV) I do not know anyone who doesn't enjoy a good night of sleep. God intends for His heirs to get uninterrupted sleep and to get up feeling refreshed every day. Isn't that neat? He tells us to put our confidence in Him. God is bigger and mightier than anything the world throws at us to rob us of His rest. We do not have to fear what the world fears because our God and Father is from another world—the world made up of miracles!

God lets His light shine on His children. He tells us in Psalm 27:1, "The Lord is my light and my salvation-whom shall I fear? The Lord is the stronghold of my life-of whom shall I be afraid?" (NIV)

So often, sickness attacks the body of a believer, so God included healing scriptures in His Word. It is very important to stay close to Jesus. In Luke 6:19, "the people all tried to touch Him, because power was coming from Him and healing them all." There is no sickness that God cannot heal. Just saying the name of Jesus is powerful. If you are suffering from a broken heart, God will heal you. He tells us in Psalms 147:3 "He healeth the broken in heart, and bindeth up their wounds." (KJV)

God will go above and beyond what we ask for, but how far God goes is based upon the degree of power that you, as the believer, hold. You must understand that Living in the Land of Miracles is not all there is. There are degrees or levels of power working in the believer. Christ tells us in

Ephesians 3:20 "Now unto him that is able to do exceeding abundantly above all that we ask or think, according to the power that worked in us." (KJV) This should encourage you to pray more and to trust in God for the answer. God is trying to teach the believer that He is a God that is more than enough.

When you are in need of a breakthrough in a situation, God wants you to expect it to happen. God's children can serve Him with expectations. When I am preparing God's message for the church, I prepare it expecting something great to happen. When I attend a service, I go expecting. When I pray for people, I pray with expectation. When I give tithes and offerings, I do it expecting a good return. There are the super righteous that get offended when you talk about expecting a good return on money given for the Lord's work. Let's look at what God has to say about your money. Luke 6:38 says, "Give, and it will be given to you. A good measure, pressed down, shaken together and running over, will be poured into your lap. For with the measure you use, it will be measured to you." (NIV) This verse covers so many of the "all things" God talks about in Matthew 6:33. As you give in prayer, you receive; as you give in love, as you give your money, you receive back. God wants the believer to "freely give" in all areas of their Christian life and God will freely give back!

Proverbs 3:9-10 says to "Honor the Lord with your wealth, with the first fruits of all your crops; then your barns will be filled to overflowing, and your vats will brim over with new wine." (NIV) God will then open the way to pour out His blessings on you. If you are a giver, get ready, because God's got a blessing coming your way! When you live in the Land of Miracles, you can expect great things to happen.

Be obedient to the Word of God. When you live in obedience to God's Word, it helps you to keep doubt out of your vocabulary. Doubt will take you out of the Land of Miracles. Mark 11:23-24 says, "I tell you the truth, if anyone says to this mountain, 'Go, throw yourself into the sea', and does not doubt in his heart but believes what he says will happen, it will be done for him. Therefore I tell you, whatever you ask for in prayer, believe that you have received it, and it will be yours." (NIV) All God is asking us to do is believe that He can do what His Word says He can do.

As we look at Peter's life, even though he had failed God, he still knew who he was in Christ. He knew he lived and walked in the Land of Miracles. In Matthew 14, Jesus was going to the disciples by walking on the water. Peter saw Him and in verse 28 said, "Lord if it is you, tell me to come to you on the water. Jesus said 'Come.'" (NIV) Peter's faith had already been aroused. When Peter realized he was capable of walking on the water, he did it on the Word of God. When he heard Jesus say "come", he stepped out of the boat and was successful in doing the impossible. In the same manner, every believer has within him the ability, as well as the power, to do the impossible as long as he does it on the Word of God. Taking God at His Word is what separates believers from victory or defeat. There was only one disciple who had the courage to step out and do what no other human had ever done on planet earth. Peter left all the other disciples in the boat crying in fear. What separated Peter from all the others is that he knew with God all things were possible.

God wants miracle workers, and the miracle workers are you and me. It is up to the believers who are alive today to step out on God's infallible Word and be water-walkers. Was what Peter did risky? Yes! No one else had ever even tried walking on the water, but Peter took God at His Word. Peter knew he lived his life in the Land of Miracles! By faith, he saw himself walking on the water. Every believer should take a picture in their minds of what they want to see God do. Then start believing God to develop in their lives what they see by faith and begin talking like they already have it. Why should every child of God do this? Because you live in the Land of Miracles! Because God loves us, because you enjoy who you are in Christ, and because you delight yourself in the Lord and He will give you the desires of your heart (Psalms 37:4). Isn't it neat being a child of the King?! You can say with authority that in all things we are more than conquerors through Him that loves us.

Now let us take a look at David when He was but a boy. In 1 Samuel 17:17, David's father instructed him to take food to his brothers who were getting ready for battle with the Philistines. In verse 23, as he was talking with them, Goliath the "giant" Philistine champion stepped out to intimidate the Israelite men, and his intimidation worked in verse 24. They all ran from him in great fear. Well — everyone but David. David knew who he was in Christ. He knew he walked and lived in the Land of Miracles. David said to Saul in verse 32, "Let no one lose heart on account of this Philistine: your servant will go and fight him." (NIV) And in verse 37, "The Lord who delivered me from the paw of the lion and the paw of the bear will deliver me from the hand of this Philistine." (NIV) David was telling Saul —

"Now look! I know who I am in Christ. Listen, Saul, no weapon formed against me shall prosper (Isaiah 54:17) and I know that I can do all things through Christ which strengthens me (Philippians 4:13). Please understand, Saul, the Lord is my helper and I will not fear what man shall do unto me (Hebrews 13:6). Saul, maybe you do not understand all there is to understand, but my God is going before me and He is fighting for me as He did in Egypt before their very eyes (Deuteronomy 1:30)."

It does not make any difference how big the giant is that may be holding you back or even stopping you. God will go before you and help you win your battle...*if* you do it in the same way David did. In 1 Samuel 17:45, (NIV) David said to the Philistine, "You come against me with sword and spear and javelin, but I come against you in the name of the Lord Almighty, the God of the armies of Israel, whom you have defied." David defeated the giant that stood before him. He knew in his heart that victory over the battle was just beyond the giant. David included the name of Jesus in his battle to defeat the giant. There is power in the name of Jesus. You can stand strong in any situation in your life if you have Jesus in your heart. Jesus comes into your heart when you sincerely invite him into your heart to forgive you of your sins. When you do this, Jesus comes into your heart and you become a part of the family of God! When this takes place in your life, you become a candidate for greater works.

Chapter 3

Your Assignment is Greater Works

John 14:12 says, "Verily, verily, I say unto you, he that believeth on me, the works that I do he shall do also; and greater works than these shall he do; because I go unto my father." (KJV)

What an assignment God has given to you as His child! I want, in this life, to see my children do better than my wife and I have done. Any parent wants the best for his children. Even though God is so much greater than His children, He wants to see us do greater works than He did while He walked on planet earth. In doing greater works, God means <u>more</u> works than He did. He was on earth as a man for such a short time, so His works here on earth were limited by time. On the other hand, God has allotted you more time on earth so you will be able to accomplish more than He did while you are here on earth. Notice how God is speaking to you in His word. He opens verse 12 with "verily, verily." He wants you to pay close attention to what He has to say.

God has a plan for mankind and His plan includes you as a believer. He has empowered you to do whatever He lays upon your heart to accomplish. God will never ask you to do anything that cannot be done. Always remember, with God all things are possible, and He has told you that you can do the impossible, as long as He gets the glory.

The only way greater works are possible is through the name of Jesus. He sits at the right hand of His father, the place of power, interceding or praying for you. It is from there He enables you to do the greater works. No matter the circumstances, never count yourself out so long as you have Jesus praying for you. God is a God of more, not a God of less. He will go above and beyond anything you can ask for or anything you can imagine. God tells us in Ephesians 3:20, "Now unto Him that is able to do exceeding abundantly above all that we ask or think, according to the power that worketh in us,…"(KJV)

As always, there is a condition on how you receive from God. He tells you, "Here, according to the power you have in you." Here again God's plan is to empower you to do what He calls you to do. He tells you in Acts 1:8 that "…ye will receive power, after that the Holy Ghost is come upon you: and ye shall be witnesses unto me both in Jerusalem, and in all Judea, and in Samaria, and unto the uttermost part of the earth." (KJV)

God by His Holy Spirit equips you with His power. The very spirit of God takes up residence in you. Wow! There has never been nor ever will be any power equivalent to the power that indwells you, the true believer. In order for you to fulfill your assignment in life that God has given you, it will take the working power of the Holy Spirit. Notice the assignment—"Ye shall be witnesses." God is revealing your assignment, or in this case, your *duty*. First and foremost, your duty is found in James 1:22. "Be ye doers of the Word, and not hearers only, deceiving your own selves." (KJV) If you are truly born again, God's power is working within you to help or empower you to become a doer of the Word. A doer of the Word is a person who is lining his life up with the Word of God (the Bible). It isn't always fun doing this, but if you are serious about serving God, there is something within you driving you to become everything God's word says you are to be. And that "something" is Jesus! You cannot be a witness for Jesus unless you are always turning your ways to God's ways— Ouch! This sometimes can be painful to the flesh, so God encourages you by telling you that you can do all things through Christ who gives you strength (Philippians 4:13). Isn't it neat—God has an answer for everything!

We are serving a God that we cannot see with our eyes. For some this creates a problem, but for a truly born again believer, this is not a problem. You find in 2 Corinthians 5:7 how you are to follow Christ; it is by faith not by sight. You can have all the faith in the world and not see any results from your faith. This poses a problem to many believers because they want to sit back and tell everyone about all their faith and about what God is going to do. A faith person is not a person who just sits back. With faith you must have action. Without action, your faith is dead. James 2:17 tells us, "…Faith by itself, if it is not accompanied by action is dead." (NIV) You have to do something to activate your faith. God's Word is powerful only when followed by action.

Allow me to give you an example. You can resist the devil all day long, but without submission to God's will, your works are dead works. James 4:7 says, "Submit (an action word) yourselves, then, to God. Resist the devil and he will flee from you." (NIV) Doing what God's Word says to do will remove the devil from your circumstance. Then you can post "No Vacancy, Devil!" on your home, your car, your children, your school, on everything that belongs to you, and the devil has to leave, running from you! Ephesians 4:27 says, "Neither give place to the devil." (KJV) God has given us our assignment and part of the assignment is to defeat the devil. When you post "No Vacancy, Devil" in your life, you are acknowledging that God is taking care of you and there is no room for the devil. God tells us in Proverbs 3:6 "In all your ways acknowledge Him and He will make your paths straight." (NIV) Always include Jesus in all that you do. Never fail to confess your need for Him in your daily life. Greater works come easier as you include or confess Jesus every day! Living in the Land of Miracles guarantees your success in God's assignment for you!

Even though we know who we are in Christ, there are challenges that come our way which require a lot of courage. There are times that it takes a lot of courage to obey God's Word. As in Ezra 10:4, God's Word encourages you to "rise up; this matter is in your hands. We will support you, so take courage and do it." (NIV) The Holy Spirit will provide the courage to rise up and deal with a difficult situation. Deuteronomy 31:6 tells you to "Be strong and courageous. Do not be afraid or terrified because of them, for the Lord your God goes with you; He will never leave you nor forsake you." (NIV) You can be strong; you can be courageous! Your circumstance does not have to hold you hostage; you do not have to allow fear to overwhelm you. You do not have to give in to depression or oppression. You really can be courageous because of who you have with you…"the Lord your God goes with you! He will never leave you nor forsake you." (Deut. 31:6 — NIV) Glory to God! God is with you right now…isn't that neat?! This is how we can go through situations that appear impossible.

This, many times, could be a case when <u>standing</u> <u>firm</u> on God's Word is an <u>active faith</u>. As crazy as this sounds, there are times when you "stand firm in the faith"! You don't move! This often gives God time to work things out for you! So often we must pass through these times on our way to achieving greater works. It is in these times that our confidence must be in Christ. This is why He encourages us by what He has to say about us in Phillipians 1:6, "Being confident of this very thing, that He which hath begun a good work in you will perform it until the day of Jesus Christ." (KJV) As long as you never forget who you are in Christ and what you can accomplish as a child of God, God will move a mountain in your life to accomplish His will for your life. Proverbs 3:26 encourages you..."For the Lord shall be thy confidence, and shall keep thy foot from being taken." (KJV) Never forget that Living in the Land of Miracles is a safe place to be when things around you seem to be falling apart.

Nahum 1:7 says, "The Lord is good, a strong hold in the day of trouble; and He knoweth them that trust in Him." (KJV) God wants you to cast your cares upon Him so He can see that your trust is in Him. When you do this, you activate the intervening power of God in your life. Ephesians 1:19 says "...His incomparably great power for us who believe. That power is like the working of His mighty strength." (NIV) The power that God used to raise Christ from the dead shows that God has the power to defeat all the trials of life. God's power is us-ward; God makes His power available to you! His power is what makes you successful in whatever your assignment may be.

God hand-picked you to fulfill His plan for you in your lifetime. In John 15:16, Jesus said, "Ye have not chosen me, but I have chosen you, and ordained you, that ye should go and bring forth fruit, and that your fruit should remain." (KJV) You have been chosen to proclaim the message of Jesus Christ. Jesus says in John 20:21 "...as My Father hath sent me, even so send I you." (KJV) God chose you to bear fruit by having good Christian character and the fruits of the Spirit. When you are living in obedience to God's word, you are abiding in Christ. The results are spiritual fruit. The end result to bearing fruit is drawing the strength and authority to live in victory day by day. When you are walking at this level with Christ, you can receive the things of God which help you in your assignment. Christ assures you in John 14:13-14 "And whatsoever ye shall ask in My Name, that will I do, that the Father may be glorified in the Son." Verse 14 "If ye shall ask anything in My Name, I will do it." (KJV) Isn't this awesome?! Jesus said to ask in His Name and He will do it. This is what validates Living in the Land of Miracles.

There are promises all through the Bible with your name on them. Being a child of the King gives you the right to stake your claim on God's promises, so serve God with all your heart, give Him all of yourself and enjoy this life in the blessings of God, your Savior! John 15:7 says, "If ye abide in me, and my words abide in you, ye shall ask what ye will and it shall be done unto you." (KJV) This is what every born-again believer can have in their relationship with Jesus Christ. My prayer is that everyone who reads this book will get within their heart that with God all things are possible. Living in the Land of Miracles is God's desire for you, so He can show the world Himself through you. What a God!

Chapter 4

God will Direct You in Your Assignment

Letting God take control of our daily walk with Him requires a change in the way we are accustomed to living our lives. First and foremost it takes a change in the way we think. With God controlling us, we must include God in our thought life. When we include God in our thoughts and in our decisions we make throughout the day, it opens the door for God to direct our every step. Psalm 37:23 tells us "The steps of a good man are ordered by the Lord, and he delighteth in his way." (KJV) This I call walking by faith because I'm putting my life into the hands of the living God, and in doing this, I'm trusting God (whom I cannot see) to direct my path. In doing this, I am acknowledging God in my life. As you and I do this, we are lining our lives up with the Word of God. Proverbs 3:5-6 tells us to…"Trust in the Lord with all your heart and lean not on your own understanding; in all your ways acknowledge Him and He will make your paths straight." (NIV) It may be difficult not to lean on your own understanding, but God wants us to put our trust in Him.

When God is directing our path, He is constantly "restoring us." This means that when we fall, He picks us up and cleans us up. Psalm 23:3 tells us "He restoreth my soul: He leadeth me in the paths of righteousness for His Name's sake." (KJV) You can be successful in your walk with

God while He is leading you in the "paths" of righteousness. Notice the word "paths" in Psalm 23:3. There are many ways or paths we could go, but God keeps us in the way we should go.

God's leading guides us to a place of safety as well as to growth in spiritual things. Psalm 32:8 says "I will instruct thee and teach thee in the way which thou shalt go; I will guide thee with mine eye." (KJV) This promise is to every believer who will put their trust in God, who has within themselves a "teachable spirit", who enjoys walking in obedience to His word. Allowing God to do this in your life produces a life of peace and joy, which belongs to every believer who lives in the Land of Miracles. We create this atmosphere in our lives by our relationship with Jesus Christ, and then by the words that we speak. Always go to the Word of God to see what God says about you, then let

God's words flow through you by saying, "I can do all things through Christ which strengtheneth me." (Phil. 4:13) (KJV) Living in the Land of Miracles is a result of God's strength in you.

How big is your God? The way you live is a reflection of the size of your God. The way you deal with adversity is an indication of the size of your God. Your faithfulness in church attendance and your giving of yourself, as well as your finances to further the Kingdom of God, is a reflection as to the size of your God. Your obedience to God's Word is a reflection of the size of your God. I want to remind you that as a child of God, you can live each day in a way that reflects the fact that you follow "the God" who is big enough to take care of any need that will ever be in your life!

God has put within us the things He knew we would need here on earth. He reveals His plan for us in 2 Peter 1:3 "...according as His divine power hath given unto us *all things* (italics mine) that pertain unto life and godliness, through the knowledge of Him that hath called us to glory and virtue." (KJV) Through God's "divine power" He gives you "all things" that pertain to life and godliness. In researching the word "divine," I discovered God was truly instilling within us the things we need right now on earth.

Webster's Dictionary Modern Revision reveals what God is saying about "divine power." Divine means *holy - belonging to or proceeding from God* which means we have "holy power" which means strength, energy, ability, authority, and that you are a moving force! WOW! Through the word divine, God has given you "holy strength" which means "quality of being strong."

Proceeding from the word "devine," we are full of holy vigor, which means we have an active strength; this is the ability as well as the strength to get back up after we have been knocked down.

Another ability proceeding from <u>divine</u> power is "holy toughness" which means not easily broken and able to endure hardship. This quality is very important to the believer because the Bible warns us that we must be able to endure to the end. Mark 13:13 informs you that "...he that shall endure unto the end shall be saved." (KJV) You have a divine spirit of endurance within your innermost being, and this should encourage even the doubting believers!

Holy brightness, which means we are full of light, is another quality proceeding from the words "<u>devine power</u>," which we have! Isaiah 2:5 says, "...let us walk in the light of the Lord." (NIV) Child of God, you are a part of this light that burns brightly in this dark world. (Isn't that neat!?)

Another quality proceeding from the words "divine power" is "holy maintenance" which means God is slowly and surely making you more like Him, grooming you, getting you ready for heaven. Philippians 1:6 "...being confident of this very thing that He which hath begun a good work in you will perform it until the day of Jesus Christ." (KJV)

"Holy ability," which is *power,* is another quality proceeding from the words "devine power." Acts 1:8 says, "...you shall receive power when the Holy Ghost comes upon you, and you will be my witness." (NIV) God speaks of your receiving power. This enables you to enjoy the "all things" He mentions in 2 Peter 1:3, (KJV), some of which we are discussing in this chapter.

Another quality proceeding from the words "divine power" is "divine holy faculty," which means mental or physical ability. Second Timothy 1:7 says, "For God hath not given us the spirit of fear; but of power, and of love, and of a sound mind." (KJV) God has given you divine mental ability. Your Bible reading becomes clearer, and the words of the Bible go to your heart where there is a better understanding of God's words. Suddenly you find you are reading God's words with a better under-standing, and you can physically witness more effectively. You suddenly realize you have a renewed strength in serving God. Isaiah 40:31 says, "But they that wait upon the Lord shall renew their strength, they shall mount up with wings as eagles, they shall run and not be weary, and they shall walk and not faint." (KJV)

Serving God takes on a whole new meaning. Suddenly you discover you have another quality as a result of God's divine power. This is a renewed "holy authority," which means "the right to command." You realize you are invested with power and as Peter proclaimed in Acts 3:6 "...such as I have I give thee: In the Name of Jesus Christ of Nazareth rise up and walk." (KJV) You discover you have the same boldness and confidence that Peter had in speaking to the lame man. The words God used in John 14:12 take on a new meaning "...he that believeth on me, the works that I do shall he do also, and greater works than these shall he do because I go to my Father." Verse 13, "And whatsoever ye shall ask in my Name, that will I do, that the Father may be glorified in the Son." (KJV) These things are what Living in the Land of Miracles is all about.

God is no respecter of persons, and what He says He will do, He will do!

Another divine quality proceeding from God to you is His faithfulness extended to us. Psalm 89:1 says, "…will I make known thy faithfulness to all generations." (KJV) God will be just as faithful to you as He has been to every believer from Adam and Eve to you right now.

His "sufficiency" is another divine quality that proceeds from God to you. Second Corinthians 3:5 says, "Not that we are sufficient of ourselves to think anything as of ourselves, but our sufficiency is of God."(KJV) God is enough! He is all that you will take Him for. There is nothing He does not know about you and He is working on your behalf right now, looking out for you!

God instills within us "fulfillment," another of His divine qualities. Matthew 5:6 says, "Blessed are they which do hunger and thirst after righteousness, for they shall be filled." (KJV) God will fill you just as full of Him as you want to be. He tells us to draw nigh to Him and He will draw nigh to you. See James 4:8

When you are Living in the Land of Miracles, you have an enemy that wants to move in on your territory and rob you of your position. So God has instructed you what to do in His Word. Ephesians 4:27 instructs you "…not to give the devil a foothold (or place)." (NIV) The devil has been around a lot longer than you have, so he knows every trick to use to overthrow you. He is always looking to see where we are the most vulnerable at any given moment.

There are times in everyone's lives that we must deal with circumstances that weaken us physically. When we become physically weak, our emotions become open to the attacks of the mind. When this occurs, it can affect our spiritual walk with God, which is the devil's number one priority in this life. When this happens, you must know what to do because spiritually you are in a crisis situation. This is where some knowledge of God's Word can help you through a crisis situation. Proverbs 3:6 instructs you to "acknowledge God in all your ways and He will make your paths straight." (NIV)

Get God involved in your crisis and He will work things out for your best interests. When you bring God into your situation, you find it easier to do what He tells you to do. 1 Peter 5:7-8 says, "…Cast *all* (italics mine) your anxiety on Him because He cares for you. Be self-controlled and alert. Your enemy, the devil, prowls around like a roaring lion looking for someone to devour…" Verse 9, "…Resist him, standing firm in the faith." (NIV) This is very important! In resisting the devil, you must at all times stand firm in the faith.

God has given you several examples in His Word of what can happen to believers when they do not stand firm in the faith. Second Timothy 4:10 tells us that "...Demas hath forsaken me, having loved this present world, and is departed." (KJV) In this case, Demas was overthrown by the devil because he refused to give up his love for the things of this world. He found himself in a crisis situation, the devil was attacking his soul, and the final result was that Demas deserted in the face of the enemy, giving up his position in the Land of Miracles. He found himself pursuing his own imaginations.

When you begin to pay more attention to the negative circumstances going on in your life than to what God's Word has to say about them, your focus becomes misdirected and this can lead to a spiritual crisis in your life that can cause you to lean more to the world's ideas. This is why you must be self-controlled and alert, which means to "stay focused" on who you are in Christ and where your final destination will be, which is heaven. Keeping this in your mind will help you to stay focused on Christ. Always remember - heaven is a real place!

John 14:2 reminds us "In my Father's house are many mansions: if it were not so, I would have told you. I go to prepare a place for you," Verse 3 "And if I go and prepare a place for you, I will come again, and receive you unto myself; that where I am, there ye may be also." (KJV) A place is being prepared for you in another dimension, which is heaven, if you can stay focused on who you are in Christ.

Judas was a man who lived and worked in the Land of Miracles, but his thoughts were misdirected, causing him to lose his focus on who he was in Christ. Luke 22:3-6 says, "Then Satan entered Judas, called Iscariot, one of the twelve. And Judas went to the chief priest and the officers of the temple guard and discussed with them how he might betray Jesus. They were delighted and agreed to give him money. He consented and watched for an opportunity to hand Jesus over to them when no crowd was present." (NIV) Judas was seduced by greed even though he had been warned of the consequences of sin by Christ Himself. Judas had lost his focus; he had forgotten that Christ demands loyalty! Christ gave Judas opportunity after opportunity to repent, but he refused to repent. His failure to repent resulted in a heart that became hardened. When you go too long without repenting, you will become spiritually blind and you will begin to rationalize your thinking. Judas was able to justify his actions in his own mind, which resulted in Judas taking his own life.

Demas and Judas gave up their positions with Christ because their focus was misdirected. They failed to cast "their cares" upon Christ; instead they became the god of their own lives, forgetting who they were in Christ. They both could have been saved from the battle they found themselves in if they had remained focused on Christ. John 14:7 says, "If you remain in me and my words remain in you, ask whatever you wish and it will be given to you." (NIV)

Demas and Judas failed to ask God for help. They failed to examine themselves. Second Corinthians 13:5 instructs you to "Examine yourselves, whether ye be in the faith, prove your own selves. Know ye not your own selves how that Christ is in you, except you be reprobate." (KJV) Examining yourself is your responsibility in order to see if you are everything God expects you to be. Living in the Land of Miracles requires obedience to the Word of God.

First John 3:22 reminds us that we can receive from Him anything we ask because we obey His commands and do what pleases Him. This is the place God wants you to be, so He can show Himself to you. According to the Bible we are the generation that will witness the return of Christ. In the meantime, we must hang in there and serve God with all our might, because it will be worth it all when we see Jesus!

He's coming soon; meanwhile, grow in grace and in the knowledge of our Lord and Savior Jesus Christ. To Him be glory both now and forever. Amen.

About the Author

Gary Parsons grew up in a small town and was raised in a Christian home, but it wasn't until later in his life that he accepted Christ. God had an amazing plan for Gary. God miraculously transformed a "bug scrubber" into a man with a mission and a message. Gary was called to share the message of God's Word to the people, and he has dedicated his life to sharing that message with everyone he meets. Today, Gary pastors a church, hosts a television program, and has an Internet site to fulfill God's mission of sharing the message. Gary has also published a book entitled <u>Get</u>

<u>This!</u> <u>This is Knowledge</u> praying it gets in the hands of many readers.

Printed in the United States
16461LVS00001B/8-109